# Swimming in God

*Daily Poems of Longing, Joy, and Love*

## TINA DATSKO DE SÁNCHEZ

*Foreword by Maren Tirabassi*

Open Waters Publishing
1300 East 9th Street
Cleveland, Ohio 44114

Published 2022.

Printed on acid-free paper.

26 25 24 23 22   1 2 3 4 5

Library of Congress Cataloging-in-Publication Data on file.
LCCN: 2021943795

ISBN 978-0-8298-1230-5 (paper)

Printed in The United States of America.

Original cover artwork by Loryn Spangler-Jones
Book and cover design by Meredith Pangrace

*For José, whose love teaches me to live.*

# CONTENTS

**Foreword**

**Preface**

**Thirty Poems of Longing (titled by first line)**

1. Oh, Beloved, your shadow is cast over
2. God, you have taken everything from me—
3. I would like to hate you for this pain
4. As sun-lit koi gasp and pile atop each other,
5. Beloved, it is a dark and cold day
6. The ineffable—that is what I thirst for.
7. As a guitar string cannot observe music
8. Today palm fronds sway in gusts of wind.
9. If Spirit breaks us open so we may wake up,
10. Beloved, shadows of palm fronds
11. Grief kept me frozen, still.
12. Night narrows the world to a candle flame
13. When my lover's face clouds over,
14. The tulips push upward, undaunted
15. The mystics who dance
16. Power and light are one—
17. Today's path leads past the koi pond,
18. A fire dances in the copper brazier
19. Like spacious atoms I cannot see,

20. In a dream, a rose thorn pierces his finger.

21. I stop for inspiration, when it beckons me

22. Purple jacarandas shed their spring snow.

23. The way sun gleams on palm fronds

24. Dear friend, you have gone ahead of me

25. When friends gather round one who feels hurt,

26. Today I feel flayed—skin peeled back,

27. In the dark engine room of the mind,

28. Blue tides swell upon a gold sand beach,

29. A blue-tailed bird braces a palm nut between feet

30. As a hibiscus bud opens to the sun,

## Thirty Poems of Joy

1. As if the ocean were playing catch with itself,

2. That cluster of five waxy needles—

3. Like a wine glass that lives only

4. In my dream I am cast opposite

5. Like an Egyptian jewel of emerald and gold,

6. Swimming again in the jade lake of childhood,

7. What bliss is music! Those finger runs

8. At our Bolivian friend's wedding to his Vietnamese bride,

9. What if prayer is like a tree?

10. The *nafs* Bly spoke about, the soul's greed

11. The goodness of life is not blocked out

12. The spider's zip line shines white in the sun,

13. What bliss is a circle of friends! Last night

14. We watch our friend unroll drawings and tack them to the wall—

15. When the inner sergeant rants that all must be

16. That ultimate joy is only in the wind

17. Some days sunlight glowing through

18. The unnamed need—this hunger burns in us

19. My job as a poet is to remind you

20. The bread and wine we hunger for is love.

21. This blissful cool day with fog

22. My mother crosses the plaza of the WWII monument,

23. This hallowed time—October. Brush fires

24. By jack-o'-lantern light playful spirits gather;

25. Singing in the recital, I become an oboe

26. The nights lengthen; the sun retreats.

27. My lungs are so full; they tell me it's pneumonia—

28. The first peach blossoms of spring.

29. The balm of sleep is an ocean I join at night,

30. What can I say of joy? Only that it is

## Thirty Poems of Love

1. The sun begins to move closer, shedding

2. Love is the ocean, the mountain, and the sky.

3. The universe is making love to us today,

4. It takes a dancer, not that the steps are complex,

5. What holds you back? Are you afraid

6. We seem at times to change partners on the dance floor—

7. A lover who surprises is the best kind.

8. What would I give you to show my love?

9. Come swim with me in God—

10. God gave me a heart-sized diamond,

11. I want never to sing alone.

12. There are so many winds to blow the boat off course—

13. Trees throw down their own leaves,

14. Fed from pure light, the bean sprout

15. God, you have given me this thirst

16. Embers snug together, flaring red against night's chill.

17. God is such a jealous lover. Run

18. The regal irises herald

19. The lily bursting forth each year proclaims it,

20. Tender as a lover's lips on mine,

21. Some might think that dipping into the well

22. Some may think love involves earning or deserving,

23. From a high balcony, gazing out to the horizon,

24. Mist over sea and sky blurs their meeting point.

25. When your heart feels dry and stiff and hard, remember

26. In the dark of night, I thought I walked this path alone.

27. The gift of love is like tipping one heart

28. Love is much more outrageous than you can imagine.

29. Open, open, open to God. Surrender to the Beloved

30. In the candlelit hour the mystery unfolds.

## Acknowledgments

# FOREWORD

I planted a rose bush when I moved from Boston to the seacoast of New Hampshire. First non-parsonage home. The bush has had no roses for many years, probably because it needs rose food, which is poisonous to mammals and, although I'm not tempted, Willie the beagle desires it beyond all reason. His canine dream of heaven includes not milk, honey, and angels but rose bush food and many squirrels. This year two roses bloomed. And I noticed them. It was neither an abundance of blooms nor the usual six-foot tangle of bramble. It was two scarlet moments in a time of thorns. I noticed them literally because I was reading *Swimming in God*.

Tina Datsko de Sánchez invites her reader to a daily practice. Not a weekly planner. Not a much-needed sabbatical. A daily practice. For her it is a daily practice of writing poetry. For someone else it might be reading a poem a day (not a book, but a poem). It might be drinking a cup of coffee while watching the bird feeder, running a rutted road or a city treadmill, repairing cornrows in a child's hair while dreaming that child's future, continuing the pandemic ritual of deliberately washing hands with scented soap. She invites her reader to a life-changing intentionality of pausing each day. She does not define what all petals mean, but opens the possibility for each of us to recognize what in our lives are the brief, the few, the beautiful.

Tina Datsko de Sánchez invites her reader to conversation. *Swimming in God* emerged not from solitude or study, but from participation in a meditation group and from spiritual conversation with, of course, Rumi and Hafiz, but also William Strafford, Robert

Bly, Emily Dickinson. Her fully engaged conversation with these artistic partners shapes her words, poetic forms, unashamed generosity with her personal life, and bright spare evocation of nature. She welcomes us all to her colleagues who are dead poets and I am sure she hopes we may sometime meet them. More than that, she welcomes us to a process of engagement with artists. She tosses away the myth of unique, pure individualist art. She calls her readers to discover their own conversations. A circle of support may not be a meditation group; it may be a chorus, watercolor collective, writers group, toddler-and-parent play date, library mystery book club. Artistic dialogue may be with living or dead poets or memoirists, djembe players or dancers, potters or podcasters or pastry chefs.

Tina Datsko de Sánchez invites every reader to discover new parables and metaphors in her work and she is extravagant with her gifts. She gathers the poems into a sequence of days of the month, and the months into themes and seasons. Longing. Joy. Love. Every reader wanders those seasons and finds images that meet every situation in life, especially the one needed for that moment. Not wanting to give a "spoiler," I'll share an image from reading two of her forthcoming volumes from The Pilgrim Press: *Drinking Pure Light* and *Fierce Gratitude*. I replace her beautiful words with my more pedestrian ones. In one, she describes the holy Friend turning me upside down so all the junk hoarded in my pockets is shaken out. Did she know she wrote this poem for me? I lived with that self-knowledge for quite a while. And the hope. But I could not stop reading, so, on another day, she describes her partner turning a pineapple upside down to rest on its stiff leaves so the sweetness would follow gravity and fill it all. Could both these poems be about "turning upside down"? Could they both be about me? In her gifted words, yes.

Buy a pineapple. Look for a rose. Swim these poems . . . slowly, carefully.

—Maren C. Tirabassi

Maren C. Tirabassi is a pastor and writer. She has published twenty-two books, most recently, *Pitching our Tents: Poetry of Hospitality*, *Christmas Eve at the Epsom Circle McDonald's and Other Poems*, and *A Child Laughs: Prayers of Justice and Hope*.

# PREFACE

I would like to say something about how these poems came to be, in both the immediate and larger senses. For many years I have participated in the bi-weekly "Sacred Practices" meditation group at the First Congregational Church of Long Beach. In February of 2007, my friend and fellow meditator, Cathy Chambers, asked if I would contribute poetry for an artist's book to be auctioned at a fundraiser for summer day camp for inner-city kids. I told Cathy that it sounded fun, and I would give it some thought. By synchronicity, the founder of our meditation group, my friend Dr. Robert Kalayjian, loaned me a book of Rumi poems entitled *Birdsong*. As I read the Rumi poems and mulled on the artist's book idea, some inklings began to take shape.

Cathy walked me through some of the possible book styles and I fell in love with the flag book, a form that opens something like a pop-up book with individual "flags" that can house the text. The flag book felt rich, textural, and playful. I considered writing a long-ish text that could be spread out among the flags, but what felt most delightful was to write a series of short, related poems that could each float freely on its own flag. One of Cathy's prior flag book creations had three flags down the vertical length of what would normally be a single page. The sacred number three felt like a good shape, so I calculated three flags, times ten sets of flags, for thirty poems. This felt like a fortuitous number, paralleling the days in a month.

By that time it was the beginning of Lent. At poetry conferences over the years, I had heard poets, including William Stafford and

Robert Bly, mention the value of writing poems on a daily basis—to unblock, free up, and cleanse the instrument. One of my favorite bits of writing advice comes from William Stafford, to this effect: "If you're having trouble writing, lower your standards." At a workshop, Jane Hirshfield immortalized that as: "Lower your Staffords." As a Lenten practice, I made the intention to write "Thirty Poems of Longing" on a more-or-less daily basis. I "lowered my Staffords" by making them a "flag-friendly" size of about six lines each.

Here is where Rumi presented himself as a teacher: "When the student is ready, the master appears." I was reading *Birdsong* each morning, and Rumi's voice gently urged me to have a go at it, like a gymnastics teacher spotting a beginner through her first back flips. I had been writing longer, more narrative poems, but Rumi coached me to surrender to the jewel-like intensity of a more lyric approach. As I began to look for moments of surprise in each poem, I began to see moments of surprise in each day. My experiential lens re-focused, allowing me to see such microcosmic miracles as the unspeakable beauty of sun glinting off a leaf.

I completed "Thirty Poems of Longing" in about two months, and Cathy made a beautiful artist's book inspired by Tibetan flags, which we donated to the fundraising auction. I was enjoying the experience so much that I didn't want to stop, so I made an intention to continue by writing "Thirty Poems of Joy" and then "Thirty Poems of Love." A composer friend, Stan DeWitt, set some of the poems to music as "Seven Songs of Longing," which I was able to sing at church in August 2007 and at my voice recital in November 2007. When my friend Megan Monaghan heard the songs, she told me they reminded her of Hafiz. She loaned me her copy of *The Subject Tonight is Love,* and Hafiz began team-teaching me with Rumi.

Though I have had a mystical nature since childhood, the poetic approaches I was exposed to during college and graduate school emphasized the tangible, natural world to such an extent that I came away feeling poetry was not a place for either politics or religion. What it took for me to get beyond my own prejudice was a combination of a supportive meditation group and an experience of grieving the loss of a dear friend.

In November 2004, my childhood friend Kathryn Hogue was murdered. We had shared a closeness that made us honorary sisters. Her sudden disappearance from my life brought intense, painful, and often confusing emotions. As shock gave way to grief, I found myself feeling as though I had died along with her. It took much longer than I'd imagined to process the emotions. In February 2007, when I began writing these poems, I discovered I was writing my way back into life. The movement of emotion from within onto the page had a cleansing and healing effect. Here also was a kinship to Rumi, who is said to have experienced an outpouring of poetry after the death of his beloved friend Shams of Tabriz.

As well as teachers, I have now come to experience Rumi and Hafiz as friends. Sometimes they are like rascally elder brothers who delight in putting their younger sister up to no good. From them I have learned to write with abandon and with confidence that, in my deepening thirst, is the nourishing drink itself. As the poems appeared, another surprising friend showed up to walk with me. From a very different time and place, she brought another layer of gentle playfulness. I discovered her nearby when I penned the line, "I stop for inspiration, when it beckons me . . . ." This sweet sojourner is of course Emily Dickinson.

As these poems have been my daily traveling companions, my hope is that they can become yours, too.

—Tina Datsko de Sánchez

"Enlightenment is when the wave
realizes it is the ocean."
—Thich Nhat Hanh

Thirty Poems of Longing

**1**.

Oh, Beloved, your shadow is cast over
me from the candle that you are.

Its gasp is my gasp, to swallow in
this universe and grow immense.

Consume me, Beloved, that this tallow
blaze in joining your light.

**2.**

God, you have taken everything from me—
my skin, my bones, my hair, my love.

God, I am nothing but your breath
which lifts me like a kite.

God, in deepest night your music stirs me
to know you, throat open, singing.

**3.**

I would like to hate you for this pain
in life—broken body, broken dreams.

I push you away and run from you.
Yet you cover me with your kisses

in each golden dawn, each dew-drenched
lily, each sky lark dropping like a lightning bolt.

**4.**

As sun-lit koi gasp and pile atop each other,
such is my hunger for you, Beloved.

But I would sit in the water lily, await its opening,
to know you unfurling in my heart.

This banner that whips and floats like a wing
is where I live, and love meets me.

## 5.

Beloved, it is a dark and cold day
when you are not with me.

Then as the fog of illusion burns off,
I see you were always there ready to warm me.

Beloved, let my spirit find its wings
to climb above clouds and join your light.

**6.**

The ineffable—that is what I thirst for.
Somehow it is present and not present.

In the dawn with its liquid amber light.
In the fresh peach juice of your kisses.

Life surrounds me and it is so full,
my very being aches with joy and sings.

## 7.

As a guitar string cannot observe music
but must be music, let me vibrate with pure Love.

As a dancer unites with the beat of the drum,
let my limbs unite with Love's hands calling the dance.

Blow into me, great soul, though I am but a
hollow reed, let hidden truths sing through me.

**8.**

Today palm fronds sway in gusts of wind.
Sometimes Love is a gentle, lazy lapcat.

Yesterday Love thundered and drenched me
in summer showers. I danced in its torrents.

At night God holds me in wolfen jaws
and shakes me awake to recall eternity.

**9.**

If Spirit breaks us open so we may wake up,
oh, to burst open like the lily bud
and trumpet in the dawn.

The poppy opens wide, an orange target with
yellow heart. The bee delights, bathing in its pollen.
Let me be the poppy, and the bee.

**10.**
Beloved, shadows of palm fronds
play across the patio.

Shadow and light seem so distinct
in their dance along river stones.

If you are light and I am shadow,
does not shadow exist because of light?

## 11.

Grief kept me frozen, still.
But the Lord of Dance warms me now,
demands motion. Can I jump for joy?

Even the rosebushes, amputated
of all life, send out new red stems
and lift yellow heads, mirroring the sun.

**12.**

Night narrows the world to a candle flame
and these flame-orange tulips in a vase.

The windows mirror back the room,
the world outside curtained in black.

I could lid my eyes with black, and let orange
flame within, for you are all places, Beloved.

**13.**

When my lover's face clouds over,
it saddens me

and reminds me of when my Creator
feels distant and silent.

Both lover and Creator mirror me,
for I am the one who's wandered off.

**14.**

The tulips push upward, undaunted
by the briefness of their blooming.

Each day they stretch themselves
to be closer to the light.

How do they do it when their stems are cut?
Surely they've learned to drink from the well of spirit.

## 15.

The mystics who dance
know that laughter is the key.

The wind doesn't really blow the sail;
it sucks the boat forward.

Desire is everything; that difference
of air pressure lifts the bird's wing.

**16.**

Power and light are one—
to see clearly, to know

and love deeply. This is the blade
that is at once a torch

held high in the night. Shadows turn
and we see the dancing faces of friends.

**17.**
Today's path leads past the koi pond,
the sun and I midway in our journeys.

Squiggles of red, orange, white, gold—
like paint on canvas come to life—

raucously make living art. Is this what
our creator sees? Are we brush and pigment?

**18.**

A fire dances in the copper brazier
and embers float upward in the night sky.
Their passion makes them lighter than air.

They do not think how to reach God
but only burn as brightly
as they can this night.

**19.**

Like spacious atoms I cannot see,
my dear friend's spirit can be present—

the living world not as real as it seems
and the spirit realm more real than imagined.

They interlace like the scents of rain
and jasmine mingling on the night air.

**20.**

In a dream, a rose thorn pierces his finger.
An old woman tears off soft
yellow petals, wraps them round the thorn.

Is this the sacrifice of beauty for protection?
Or beauty's tender balm
salving again his woundedness?

**21.**

I stop for inspiration, when it beckons me
like a lover to taste its rich flesh.

There is no moment but this one
and there never will be.

Death, come sweetly. Let your juice
drip down the sides of my chin.

**22.**

Purple jacarandas shed their spring snow.
In the backyard, the mower whines—
summer imminent in gold-glinting sun.

How good it is to be alive and relish
seasons like the courses of a meal.
Creator, you have set your table richly.

**23.**

The way sun gleams on palm fronds
tells me you are near, Beloved.

The rustling wind carries your perfume.
I could drink its scent forever.

Sacred wisdom, shimmer in me—
to glow in your light like a pear in the sun.

**24.**

Dear friend, you have gone ahead of me
to whatever is beyond this life.

Your eyes do not see the daylilies' saffron robes.
Your ears do not hear the chant of wind in branches.

I choose to see and hear doubly, that my heart
in longing for the Great Soul, may greet you.

**25.**

When friends gather round one who feels hurt,
we are like wolves licking wounds of mate or cubs.

Geese fly chevrons in autumn sky,
winging the arrow by taking turns.

In our mute instincts, compassion comes naturally
without our magpie greed for clutching what glitters.

**26.**

Today I feel flayed—skin peeled back,
heart a raw wound.

Beloved, come to me now, enfold me
in coolness, stillness, peace.

Put your hand on my wound and seal it
with the healing light of your grace.

**27.**

In the dark engine room of the mind,
when the gears freeze and will not turn,

let divine light be the pungent oil
that soothes the breakdown.

Great Spirit, breathe into me with your love
and fill me like a parachute.

**28.**

Blue tides swell upon a gold sand beach,
a place of peace and tranquility.

How I long to dive into your depths, Great Soul,
and in clear water see hidden truths.

Support me to rest on your breath
and float on the turquoise skin of wisdom.

**29.**

A blue-tailed bird braces a palm nut between feet
and with beak chisels it open to gulp the meat.

Intent, the bird tries several angles
to break the task into bite-size pieces.

A shimmer of blue, it wings to the palm's crest—
to be so nourished and joyful in a job complete.

**30.**

As a hibiscus bud opens to the sun,
Beloved, I open to your love.

My thirst sends down roots
beyond space and time.

And you are here, summoned by the asking—
breathless, and eager to dance.

# Thirty Poems of Joy

**1.**

As if the ocean were playing catch with itself,
the glassy waves palm me to and fro.

Snorkeling beside a lava wall that plunges deep
to white sand, I am surprised with a turtle surfacing.

Just so, to those who wait and watch
the numinous soon presents itself.

**2.**

That cluster of five waxy needles—
white pine—cuts through memory
with dewdrop clarity.

Joy is in this moment, in the crystalline
globe of the dewdrop
that opens on eternity.

**3.**

Like a wine glass that lives only
for the outpouring that fills it,

gathering with friends around a candle-lit table
opens a space, a receptacle for energy,

and Spirit, that greatest of vintages,
flows in joyously to fill it.

**4.**

In a dream I am cast opposite
a great actor and feel intimidated.

He seems aloof, and then I know him as my own Muse.
He tells me it is I who am not fully committed.

Commitment is bliss. One cannot dance
with only one foot on the dance floor.

## 5.

Like an Egyptian jewel of emerald and gold,
a green beetle flies its daily rounds, bumbling against
walls and windows—its joy undaunted.

The peace of the garden with sprinklers sparkling,
this Eden, and the bejeweled ancient magic
of winging headlong into the moment.

## 6.

Swimming again in the jade lake of childhood,
I am enveloped in simplicity and bliss.

The cool green spring-fed water
quenches body and soul.

We plunge and resurface, cycling even as our
spirits cycle through little deaths and births.

**7.**

What bliss is music! Those finger runs
up and down the keyboard expand the soul.

Poetry and dance are prayer—that awareness
of connection with life force and all beings.

Let us encircle each other with song,
our love the strength that holds us up.

**8.**

At our Bolivian friend's wedding to his Vietnamese bride,
one image emerges. After the struggle with language,
the loosening of traditions. After the feast of lobster
at orchid-festooned tables, the trilingual DJ gets us all up
to do the twist, and later the couple are embraced

by a circle of dancing friends—their beaming faces
Asian, European, African, Latino—their love cradling
the newlyweds. There is a glimpse of
possibility, of what this world could look like
if we recognize we are dancing together as one family.

**9.**

What if prayer is like a tree?

In moonlight, our roots reach deep into moist soil.
In sun and wind, our branches stretch to blossom and bear fruit.

As above, so below: roots and branches both expand.
This balance keeps the tree healthy.

The heart grows strong and mediates
all things from its flowing core.

**10.**

The *nafs* Robert Bly spoke about, the soul's greed
that gnaws on everything like an abandoned pup.

How to still the craving needs: urgency, possession, orgasm, fame?
The calm is in connection, opening the ancient door

on rusted hinges to the room of sky, peace, love—
where soul unites to soul in a grid of light.

**11.**

The goodness of life is not blocked out
by work or worry or even illness.

The goodness of life resides in each sweet breath,
the smell of warm bread, the taste of honey.

The goodness of life is always here
like a treasured book we have only to open.

**12.**

The spider's zip line shines white in the sun,
appearing and disappearing as the wind breathes.

Tall as the palm tree, it looks like a kite string
to heaven. That remarkable tensile strength—

is it only trust that allows
such passionate creative leaps into the void?

**13.**

What bliss is a circle of friends! Last night
we dined on shish-kebab and sangria.

But our real meal was joy—the playful
gathering of gypsy souls, sharing song, poetry, image.

This is the family of my birthright—those mothered
in joy where soul sparks soul.

**14.**

We watch our friend unroll drawings and tack them to the wall—
white and black chalk over terracotta, amber, woodland grounds.

Each image appears then is replaced, delighting
our senses like a sultan's banquet.

Mind and heart pleasure in tasting life, love, family,
connection, yearning—this devotion to truth in art.

**15.**

When the inner sergeant rants that all must be
ordered, structured, rigid, on time—

tell him we are off the clock.
We've gone out dancing because the planets

can only spin if we dance them into motion
with our whirling frolic and joy.

**16.**

That ultimate joy is only in the wind
tickling sun-lit palm fronds.

It is only in the color of apples, pumpkins, eggplant
in the market. Only there and everywhere.

That ultimate joy is only where I'm looking now
and only if I'm really seeing.

**17.**

Some days sunlight glowing through
green-gold leaves is too much to bear.

Some days the yearning for my lover and for God
swells the back of my throat, and I can barely breathe.

I thank God I must only endure this a human lifetime,
or surely I would catch fire and burst in a flash of white.

**18.**

The unnamed need—this hunger burns in us
with a cool white flame and turns us clear as glass.

An emptiness with gnawing teeth would consume
all as greed, lust, jealousy—so intense it drives us mad.

Bless Hafiz, our wise physician, who sets us free
by naming our need for God.

**19.**

My job as a poet is to remind you
the thirst in your throat is not just for water

or wine, and the hunger gnawing below your heart
is not just for bread or meat.

My job is to remind us both—this longing is for
communion—only to be filled by a love that is God.

**20.**

The bread and wine we hunger for is love.
God is what we thirst for.

So eat this bread and drink this wine to remember
only the Beloved can fill that empty gnawing place in us.

The God diet—when you are hungry, fill up on God;
unlimited serving is available.

**21.**

This blissful cool day with fog
pressing down like a gray woolen blanket.

We are tucked snugly in bed with God
and the whole day ahead of us—

to play games, drink hot chocolate and cuddle,
reading poems that stretch us to the edges of the universe.

**22.**

My mother crosses the plaza of the WWII monument,
her peach raincoat streaming behind her in the breeze.

The stroke that blurred planning and executing
only deepens focus on her joy in the moment.

And so we will all be marching forward on strong legs
of spirit, our doubts flapping behind till they finally let go.

**23.**

This hallowed time—October. Brush fires
choke the air with amber light.

And yet the portal to beauty remains open.
For those who know the secret watchwords,

the spirits on the other side pull back the veil
so we all can dance and sing together in God's ballroom.

**24.**

By jack-o'-lantern light playful spirits gather;
we feast on roast pork and friendship, wine and song.

Autumn harvest spreads its joy, gourds and pumpkins
ripe to bursting with the goodness of the universe

and seeds of wisdom—knowing every season and process,
every turn of the globe, is immersed in God.

**25.**

Singing in the recital, I become an oboe
played by God. My tongue and palate form
the reed as I give back what God breathes into me.

My regrets of not singing opera evaporate like
dew in morning sun. I am fully present here and now:
this moment, this flow, are all they need to be.

**26.**

The nights lengthen; the sun retreats.
We are come again to festivals of light—
menorahs, Christmas trees, twinkling lights on rooftops.

In these darkened hours, we must light candles
in each other's hearts. Gently, gently now
let the flame of joy burst forth.

**27.**

My lungs are so full; they tell me it's pneumonia—
the barrier to death paper thin as the wall of a cheap motel.

I keep hearing a growling beast on the other side
as my chest rattles.

But truly I know that even if I drown,
there's no greater joy than swimming in God.

**28.**

The first peach blossoms of spring.
Our neighbor brings them over with a tray
of chili to soothe my illness.

This immense kindness of humanity and nature,
through which God embraces me
and smiles contagious beams from a radiant face.

**29.**

The balm of sleep is an ocean I join at night,
the river of my spirit running downwards to meet the sea,
leaping over rocks with a dancer's *grand jeté*.

My spirit's laughing stream hungers for depth
and knows no bounds. At night my spirit slips
into the deepest well-spring, thirsting for God.

**30.**

What can I say of joy? Only that it is
your birthright. Consume it daily, like chocolate.

Only the drinking in of joy creates the suction,
the siphoning, to keep it welling from the heart of the universe.

You would do well to make this your job—become a miner of joy.
It is the wise fool's gold, sunlight of God's love.

# Thirty Poems of Love

**1.**

The sun begins to move closer, shedding
garments of clouds to better make love with you.

Woo the light as you may, nothing speeds the process.
All things in their own time, in their own season.

Dear one, the light within is always burning;
its bright spark illumines all manner of lovemaking.

**2.**

Love is the ocean, the mountain, and the sky.
Love is all there is and there's no escaping.

God is the great seducer and can wait as long
as it takes for you to give yourself fully.

Why resist any longer? Why not strip bare
and bathe in Love's sweetness today?

**3.**

The universe is making love to us today,
caressing our eyes with spring blossoms.

There, feel your breath tracing
the mark God's lips left on you.

The Beloved is devoted to giving us pleasure
to show how dearly we are loved.

**4.**

It takes a dancer, not that the steps are complex,
though a good sense of balance helps.

It takes a dancer to spin with this planet
while fixing one's gaze in just one spot.

It takes a dancer to move with intention,
sensing the reality that we are swimming in God.

**5.**

What holds you back? Are you afraid
of getting drunk and falling down in public?

My dear, the Beloved is the biggest drunk of all,
completely besotted and wilder than we can imagine.

So now, gulp down the cup God offers you.
Then, only then, will God hold you up on the dance floor.

**6.**

We seem at times to change partners on the dance floor—
Divorce, remarriage, or love that dies and is reborn.

Perhaps the partner is always somehow new
as we whirl into the next dance.

Does it really matter when every partner
is a stand-in, an understudy, for God?

## 7.

A lover who surprises is the best kind.
With winter at its grayest, suddenly a pink rose!

When I think I know where the boat's headed,
change course! Turn me upside down and shake me

till ideas hidden in my pocket linings
fall out on the page.

Surprise me, O God, do your wild irascible
fire dance that sets us all ablaze.

**8.**

What would I give you to show my love?
The laughing moon and dancing stars?

They are already on this page.
Would I mine for rubies and emeralds?

I would give you wide eyes and an open heart
and this strong page to wrap them in for safekeeping.

**9.**

Come swim with me in God—
my poem is water, your song is water
flowing raucously to the sea.

Come swim with me in God—
where else to be one than in God's oneness,
leaping like dolphins in the deep, laughing ocean?

**10.**

God gave me a heart-sized diamond,
said I could sell it to buy luxury and status.

But the gift is too precious to sell.
Daily I slice it in panes for a shining lantern.

And the chips, the seeds, I give to others
so they can grow their own diamond heart.

## 11.

I want never to sing alone.
I want my heart to be always vibrating

where God has grabbed hold and tuned
and strummed me like a lute.

The Beloved is a hands-on teacher,
and my voice can only float with that accompaniment.

**12.**

There are so many winds to blow the boat off course—
worries and expectations, even hormones.

You now remember the hiding place
of the key to the secret garden in your heart.

Practice turning the key, do it daily, and venture
to the verdant fertile place where love is always in bloom.

**13.**

Trees throw down their own leaves,
stand naked all winter with trust in spring green buds.

Plants seem to understand the dying back
as essential to the cycle of new growth.

They are so far ahead of us—breathing out love to us,
shaking their bright new leaves to awaken us to joy!

**14.**

Fed from pure light, the bean sprout
stands up and unfurls its first leaves.

It grew even taller during the night,
digesting the love from the sun.

We are all love's plants,
bobbing our new growth when morning comes.

**15.**

God, you have given me this thirst
in my throat, and only singing soothes it.

God, you have given me this ache
in my heart, and only loving heals it.

God, my head is spinning now, nudging me
to know I am eternally dancing with you.

**16.**

Embers snug together, flaring red against night's chill.
Our love burns brighter when we press in close together.

Touching one another, something in us remembers
we were made for this proximity.

Like cells, like exploding quivering cells,
together we form the only body God has.

**17.**

God is such a jealous lover. Run
to Earth's end and you cannot escape love's eye.

But only surrender, stand your ground
and let this wild beast engulf you.

God is such a tender lover. Dance,
and God's laughter caresses you with lily-scented air.

**18.**

The regal irises herald
the first day of spring.

They could look somber
in their purple robes.

But look closely. They are dancing
and singing as they drink in love's light.

**19.**

The lily bursting forth each year proclaims it,
as does the butterfly flashing by on white wings.

Let's not be fooled by endings—
night, winter, or death.

Eternal love is here and now,
and so will it always be.

**20.**

Tender as a lover's lips on mine,
God breathes life into me today.

My crushed lung opens, a butterfly
wet from the cocoon stretching its wings to dry.

The Beloved is patient and gentle,
creating us anew, nudging us to fly.

**21.**

Some might think that dipping into the well
each day as I do is wasteful,
that it's wise to hoard and save in case of drought.

But God's well is a flowing river underground,
an ocean, a universe. Only the foolish go thirsty,
waiting to drink in the fullness of love.

**22.**

Some may think love involves earning or deserving,
or is a goal to strive to attain.

But love is the port of embarkation
and the ship, the voyage, the ports of call,

your traveling companions and the captain; above all,
the musicians who give their art to help you dance.

**23.**

From a high balcony, gazing out to the horizon,
the view infinite, the day and possibilities infinite as well,

my soul bathes in love's turquoise expanse,
emerges cleansed and rollicking,

saying: bring me a silk garb, wine, musicians and singers,
for now is the time to dance.

**24.**

Mist over sea and sky blurs their meeting point.
Today's truths come in their softer, gentler form.

Clouds do not blot out a heart on fire with love.
The mist only makes the Beloved more tangible:

this Great Spirit swirls around my leg like a nuzzling cat,
purrs into my lungs to nest in my heart.

**25.**

When your heart feels dry and stiff and hard, remember
it is time to hold it up like an empty cup that needs filling
or toss it like a sponge into a vat of golden wine.

For like a sponge it is never our substance that matters,
but the golden wine of love that fills every nook and cranny
from the laughing vintner's infinite supply.

**26.**

In the dark of night, I thought I walked this path alone.
Then the sun reached out its golden hands
to touch me and open my eyes.

Now I see I am moving shoulder to shoulder
with seekers and pilgrims. A throng
of burning hearts, we are the body of God's love.

**27.**

The gift of love is like tipping one heart
to ignite it from the flame of the one next door.

I burn my candle late into the night
and dip my pen in it to write with golden passion.

This poem has your name on it. There is one for each of your neighbors.
Strike it against your heart, and its burning will light your way.

**28**.

Love is much more outrageous than you can imagine.
It runs naked in the streets shouting your name.
It wants everyone to know
you have been promised to the Beloved.

Love is so beautiful it will make you gasp
when you finally see the radiance of God's glowing heart,
see nothing separates you but the sheerest veil.
Choose daily to fling it wide.

**29.**

Open, open, open to God. Surrender to the Beloved
sweetly, as to the most tender lover.

The mystery can only be known to earthly senses this way.
Every day the Beloved dresses you in the fine silk of breath.

Every day the Beloved showers you with emeralds of wisdom.
Every day your treasured soul can be wedded to love.

**30.**

In the candlelit hour the mystery unfolds.

Drinking deeply, dancing with abandon, the Beloved's face before yours,

sweetly breathing life into your lungs, heart, limbs.

Now become one, no part of you outside love.

All is stillness, expanse, echoing infinity.

God moves within and your soul leaps, breathless, to bliss.

# ACKNOWLEDGMENTS

Let me begin at the beginning. I am only writing today by the grace of God. My parents, Joseph and Doris Datsko, gave their five children an upbringing enriched by the arts: music and dance lessons, arts and crafts, concerts, singing in church choir. In high school, my English teachers, Mrs. Reynolds and Dr. Swenson-Davis, challenged me to develop my writing. In college, I majored in creative writing, choreography, and psychology of creativity through the mentoring of Professor Walter Clark, Professor Vera Embree, and Professor Rudolf Arnheim. My Aunt Clara also encouraged me to embrace being a writer. And when I met my soulmate, Dr. José Sánchez-H., he became the greatest champion and co-conspirator of my creative endeavors. His are the first eyes to see each poem I write, and he patiently reads my work before it goes out into the world.

For the growth of my writing in the direction of spiritual poetry, I want to thank some of the gardeners whose care helped it flourish. The Reverend Mary Ellen Kilsby and the Reverend Libby Tigner celebrated my early attempts. The Reverend Jerald Stinson helped me to engage collaboratively with clergy. Cathy Chambers brainstormed with me on making an artist book, a project from which all of this poetry has flowed. Later, as Moderator at the First Congregational Church of Long Beach, Cathy was instrumental in my being awarded the Aaron and Maycie Herrington Pathfinder Award and being given the honorary title of Poet in Residence, both of which opened this "pathless path" before me.

The community of the First Congregational Church of Long Beach provided fertile ground in which my creative process grew deep roots. Thus rooted, poetry began to flow through me, both for liturgical use and for these volumes. The Sacred Practices meditation group, which I co-lead with Dr. Bob Kalayjian, has offered the cross-pollination of both hearing and sharing poems. I am grateful to Dr. Bob and all my fellow meditators. Gratitude also flows to others who have been part of the FCCLB community. Megan Monaghan shared with me a collection of poetry by Hafiz that scattered more seeds. Composer Stan DeWitt set seven of the poems as "Seven Songs of Longing." Additionally, Director of Music Curtis Heard set some of the poems for liturgical use. The Reverend John Forrest Douglas made a video of one of my poems.

I especially want to thank the godmothers and godfathers of these books. The Reverend Mary Scifres read *Swimming in God* and recommended I try The Pilgrim Press. The Reverend Elena Larssen spoke with and wrote a letter of introduction for me to The Pilgrim Press, as well as the foreword to *Dancing through Fire*. The Reverend Molly Baskette wrote an endorsement for me to send to the publisher and also the foreword for *Fierce Gratitude*. The Reverend Jim Burklo gave me many doses of encouragement and wrote the foreword for *Drinking Pure Light*. The Reverend Maren Tirabassi invited me to share my poetry and wrote the foreword for *Swimming in God.*

As publisher of The Pilgrim Press, the Reverend Rachel Hackenberg humbled me with her radical welcome of the four manuscripts. I am deeply grateful to her for believing in this poetry. Licensing coordinator Kathryn Martin has valiantly answered my many questions and helped me through the process. Program assistant Georgetta Thomas coordinated schedules and communications. Production coordinator Adam Bresnahan guided the manuscripts into book form. My gratitude to each of them as well.

My heartfelt thanks to my attorney Phillip Rosen for his thoughtful and generous support with the publishing agreements. Gratitude also to my friend Nancy Schraeder for her many years of encouragement and her careful proofreading. Many thanks as well to Suzanne Lyons, whose career coaching gave me the tools to implement my dreams.

# ABOUT THE AUTHOR

Tina Datsko de Sánchez is an author and filmmaker whose work won fourteen Hopwood Awards and the Los Angeles Arts Council Award. Her writing appeared in magazines and books in several countries, including *Michigan Magazine*, *Nimrod*, *Psychological Perspectives*, *Sojourners*, and *The Heroine's Journey Workbook*. Her bilingual poetry book, *The Delirium of Simón Bolívar*, published jointly by Floricanto Press and Berkeley Press with a foreword by Edward James Olmos, won the Phi Kappa Phi Award and a Michigan Council for the Arts Grant. She wrote and produced the feature documentary *Searching for Simón Bolívar: One Poet's Journey*, which premiered at the 30th Festival of Latin American Cinema in Trieste, Italy. Her poetry films aired on Sundance Channel and CNN *Showbiz Today*. She taught creative writing at the University of Michigan and screenwriting at California State University, Long Beach. She serves as Poet in Residence at the First Congregational Church in Long Beach, where she resides.

# WORKS BY TINA DATSKO DE SÁNCHEZ

## POETRY

*Fierce Gratitude*
*Drinking Pure Light*
*Dancing through Fire*
*The Delirium of Simón Bolívar* (translated by José Sánchez-H.)

## FILMS (as Writer/Producer)

*Searching for Simón Bolívar: One Poet's Journey*
*The Candle*
*Crossing the Andes*
*Robinson*
*Domitila Speaks to the Earth*
*The Pomegranate*
*The Millstone*
*My General*
*The Man of Laws*
*The Delirium*
*News for Manuela*
*The Road to the Coast*
*Rudolf Arnheim: A Life in Art*
*La Paz* (co-written with José Sánchez-H.)
*Yo no entiendo a la gente grande*

## PLAYS

*Manuelita*
*La Paz* (co-authored with José Sánchez-H.)